Learning to Read, Step by Step!

Ready to Read   Preschool–Kindergarten
• big type and easy words • rhyme and rhythm • picture clues
For children who know the alphabet and are eager to begin reading.

Reading with Help   Preschool–Grade 1
• basic vocabulary • short sentences • simple stories
For children who recognize familiar words and sound out new words with help.

Reading on Your Own   Grades 1–3
• engaging characters • easy-to-follow plots • popular topics
For children who are ready to read on their own.

Reading Paragraphs   Grades 2–3
• challenging vocabulary • short paragraphs • exciting stories
For newly independent readers who read simple sentences with confidence.

Ready for Chapters   Grades 2–4
• chapters • longer paragraphs • full-color art
For children who want to take the plunge into chapter books but still like colorful pictures.

STEP INTO READING® is designed to give every child a successful reading experience. The grade levels are only guides; children will progress through the steps at their own speed, developing confidence in their reading. The F&P Text Level on the back cover serves as another tool to help you choose the right book for your child.

Remember, a lifetime love of reading starts with a single step!

For E.T.
—J.R.

Text copyright © 2016 by Joe Rhatigan
Illustrations copyright © 2016 by Thomas Girard

All rights reserved. Published in the United States by Random House Children's Books,
a division of Penguin Random House LLC, New York.

Step into Reading, Random House, and the Random House colophon are registered trademarks
of Penguin Random House LLC.

Photograph credits: Pages 1, 9, 10–11, 12, 14, 15, 16, 18, 19, 20–21, 22, 23, 24–25, 26, 27, 30–31,
38, 39, 41, 42, 43: Courtesy of NASA. Page 13: Found on Wikimedia Commons.

Visit us on the Web!
StepIntoReading.com
randomhousekids.com

Educators and librarians, for a variety of teaching tools, visit us at RHTeachersLibrarians.com

Library of Congress Cataloging-in-Publication Data
Names: Rhatigan, Joe, author. | Girard, Thomas, illustrator.
Title: Space : planets, moons, stars, and more! / by Joe Rhatigan ;
illustrations by Thomas Girard.
Other titles: Step into reading. Step 3 book.
Description: New York : Random House Children's Books, [2016] | Series: Step
into reading. Step 3
Identifiers: LCCN 2015029603 | ISBN 978-0-553-52316-4 (trade pbk.) | ISBN
978-0-553-52317-1 (hardcover library binding) | ISBN 978-0-553-52318-8 (ebook)
Subjects: LCSH: Outer space—Juvenile literature. | Solar system—Juvenile
literature.
Classification: LCC QB602 .R48 2016 | DDC 523.1—dc23

Printed in the United States of America

20

This book has been officially leveled by using the F&P Text Level Gradient™ Leveling System.

STEP 3

READING ON YOUR OWN

STEP INTO READING®

A SCIENCE READER

SPACE

Planets, Moons, Stars, and More!

by Joe Rhatigan

illustrations by Thomas Girard

Random House 🏠 New York

What do you see
when you think of
outer space?
Strange planets?
Rocket ships?
Aliens?

Would you believe
we are all in outer space
right now?
It's true.

Earth is just a tiny part of
the universe.
Everything is part of
the universe.
That includes the planets,
the moon,
the stars,
and you!

You can see some of
the universe
in the night sky.

You can also see
part of it
during the day—
the sun!

The sun is actually a star.

It is just like

the tiny points of light

you see in the sky at night.

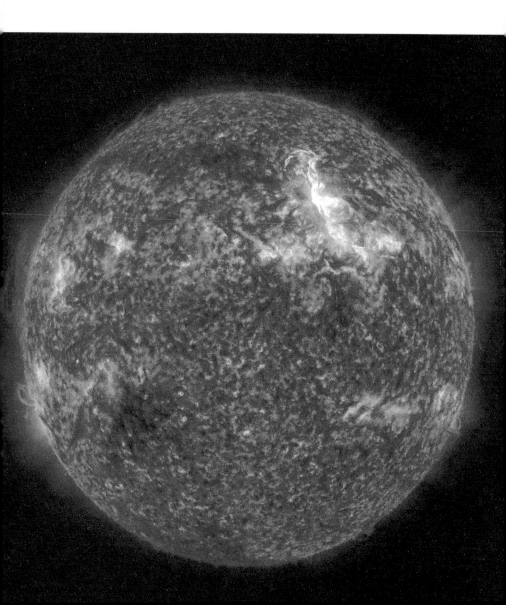

Is the sun the biggest star?

No!

It is just closer to Earth

than any other star.

Because the sun is so big,

it attracts other giant bodies

to it.

The force that attracts
smaller things to bigger things
is called gravity.

Eight planets are pulled
toward the sun.
They circle,
or orbit, it.
This space neighborhood
is called the solar system.

Mercury is the planet
closest to the sun.
It is a rocky planet
with craters and volcanoes.

Venus is the second planet
from the sun.
It is surrounded by
thick clouds.
It is the hottest and brightest
planet in the solar system.

Next is Earth—our home!
It is a rocky planet
mostly covered with water.
It is the only planet
that can support human life.
Earth has one moon.

Mars is called
the Red Planet.
It gets its red color
from the rusty iron soil.

People used to think
there were creatures on Mars,
called Martians.
Mars has *two* moons!
They are not round
like our moon.

The next four planets
are called the giant planets.
They are made of gases
or icy materials.
Each one has
many moons.

Jupiter   Saturn

Uranus   Neptune

Jupiter is a gas giant.

It is the largest planet.

It is so big that

all the other planets

could fit inside it!

Saturn is the sixth planet.

It is also a gas giant.

It is known for its
beautiful rings.

The rings are made of

ice,

dust,

and rocks.

Uranus (YUR-uh-nus)
is the seventh planet,
and an ice giant.
Uranus also has rings.
It is blue-green
and tipped on its side.

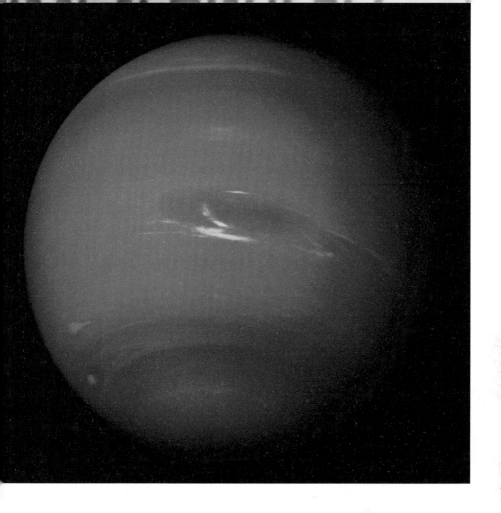

Neptune is the eighth planet.
This ice giant has wild winds
that blow 1,500 miles per hour.
Its gases make it appear
bright blue.

We used to think
there was a ninth planet,
called Pluto.
But in 2006,
scientists decided
it was too small
to be a real planet.

Ceres   Pluto   Haumea

It is now called
a dwarf planet.
The other dwarf planets are
Ceres (SEER-eez),
Haumea (how-MAY-uh),
Makemake (mah-kay-MAH-kay),
and Eris (EHR-is).

Makemake   Eris

There are other objects
in our solar system, too.
Asteroids are rocks
that orbit the sun.

There are millions of them

between Mars

and Jupiter.

Some are

hundreds of miles wide.

Others are the size

of a school bus.

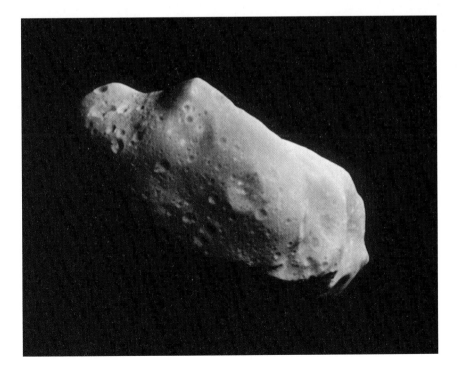

A smaller space rock
is called a meteoroid
(MEE-tee-uh-roid).
If one reaches Earth,
it is called a meteorite
(MEE-tee-uh-rite).

Comets are like
giant dirty snowballs.
They are made out of
ice, dust, and rock.

As comets get closer to the sun,

the ice changes to gas.

This makes one or more beautiful tails.

The most famous comet is

Halley's Comet.

You may see it in the sky one day

when you are all grown up!

It should appear again

in the year 2061.

Our solar system is not
the only thing in the universe.
It is part of a huge neighborhood
of other stars.
The sun is just one
of the billions of stars
in the Milky Way galaxy
(GAL-uk-see),
where we live.

A galaxy is a group of
billions of stars
orbiting a common center.
Many of these stars have
planets orbiting them.

If you can believe it,
the universe is even
bigger than that!
Outside our galaxy
are billions of other galaxies.
The universe is huge!

Let's talk more about
life on our planet.
It takes one year
for Earth to orbit the sun.
Because of Earth's position
as it orbits,
we have four seasons.

SPRING

SUMMER

Earth would not have life
without the sun.
The sun gives off light
and heat.
The sun gives energy
to plants
to help them grow.

FALL

WINTER

Earth is also spinning
like a top.
It takes twenty-four hours,
or one day,
to spin around once.

This spinning is why we have daylight . . .

. . . and nighttime.

The sun also lets us see

the moon!

The biggest object

in the night sky is the moon.

It is our closest

space neighbor.

It orbits Earth.

Once a month,

you can see the whole moon.

This is called a full moon.

At other times,

the moon

looks as if a bite has been

taken out of it.

This happens because

we see only the part

of the moon

lit up by the sun.

The different shapes

of the part of the moon

we can see

are called its phases.

How do we know all this stuff?
Astronomers
(uh-STRAH-nuh-merz)
make many discoveries!

They are scientists who study
outer space.
They use telescopes
and other tools
to learn about the universe.

Astronomers search for planets
orbiting faraway stars.
They hope to find a planet
like ours.
Maybe one day,
they will discover life
on another planet.

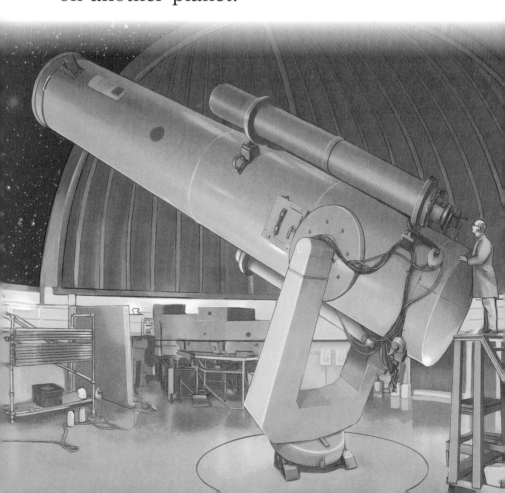

Do you wish you could
explore the universe?
Start by looking at
the night sky.

Search for constellations
(kon-stuh-LAY-shuns).
A constellation
is a group of stars
that form a pattern.

The pattern may look like

an animal,

a person,

or an object.

Astronomers learn
new things about
the universe every day.
Who knows?
Maybe one day,
you will look up
and discover something new.